100+FUCK! SWEAR WORDS

FUCK! SWEAR WORDS IN DIFFERENT LANGUAGE AND THEIR DETAILED MEANING.

BY

SCOTT KELLER

COPYRIGHTS©2023 SCOTT KELLER

The content of this book may not be reproduced, duplicated or transmitted without direct written permission from the author.

Contents

INTRODUCTION 4
   Swear words and their meanings 6
American Swear Words (US) 6
British Swear Words (UK) 11
Australian Swear Words (AU) 15
English Dirty Words 17
Irish Dirty Words 20
French Dirty Words 22
Spanish Dirty Words 25
Italian Dirty Words 27
German Dirty Words 29
Portuguese Dirty Words 31
Russian Dirty Words 33
Chinese Dirty Words 35
Japanese Dirty Words 37
Korean Dirty Words 39
CONCLUSION 41

INTRODUCTION

You won't learn these dirty words in textbooks!

Let's be honest. Whenever we learn a new language, we all get curious about how to swear. We all want to know those dirty words, the banned words, the bad words your mum would've washed your mouth out for saying.

There's something compelling about learning swear words in another language. It's almost like it gives you that insider feeling. The sense that you've got a little extra knowledge in the language that makes you closer to native speaking. Because, most of us curse – at least sometimes, right?

I think it's especially appealing, too, because it's a taboo. They're words you can't say on radio or most television, so they're a bit harder to learn and find as you're starting out in your target language.

Well, here's a great place to get you started learning those bad words. But be careful when and how you use them! If you wouldn't shout an offensive curse word in a certain situation in your native language, don't use the equivalent in another language..

SWEAR WORDS AND THEIR MEANINGS

American Swear Words (US)

The following are commonly used curse words in American English that are understood and used globally. It's likely where you should start, to get the most bang for your limited time.

- ❖ F*ck

The word f-u-c-k is one of the most widely recognized swear words in the English language. The literal f-word is a shortened version of: 'Fornication Under the Consent of the King.' Like most swear words, it did originate from a sexual reference, which is still how it's used today.

- ❖ F*ck you

Adding the word 'you' means you're directing the offense onto someone else. It's often used as a joke or when you're angry at someone else.

❖ Shit

Another meaning for shit is poo (#2), but it's often used internally when something unexpected comes up in your life. An example is if you forgot that you have a project that's due this week, you'll say 'Shit! I totally forgot about that.'

❖ Piss off

If you want someone to step away from your personal space, you can simply tell them to piss off.

❖ Dick head

You can visually imagine this swear word without too much effort I'm sure. It's a commonly used name-call that is used to describe someone who's being unfair or unjust, but it can also be with friends as a joke.

❖ Asshole

This is one of those curse words that literally describes a part of our body (in the buttocks), but is also used as a swear word.

❖ Son of a b*tch

A versatile word that can be used internally like the word 'damn' or 'shit' but can also be used to describe someone who tossed one over you.

❖ Bastard

The literal translation for a bastard is an illegitimate child or mongrel. It's used as a noun to describe someone who gave you an unpleasant experience. For example, if someone runs into you on the subway and you end up falling, calling them a bastard may be appropriate.

❖ Bitch

A common word that's not only used globally but from both males and females. According to this study, the word 'bitch' was used in 4.5 million interactions on Facebook, making it the top 5 most common swear word in the English language online.

- ❖ Damn

This is not the harshest swear word used in America and one that's said to yourself, not to harm someone else. it's most commonly used in the lower east side of the United States.

- ❖ C*nt

While this word is used as an unpleasant or stupid person in Britain and elsewhere, it's much harsher in the United States. Be careful using this, especially around women, as you may be about to enter a physical interaction quickly after.

British Swear Words (UK)

The British have one of the most original swear words. Given that it's where the English language originated from, it makes sense that they're so unique! The following British English swear words are most commonly used in the UK but are slowly being recognized around the globe.

- ❖ Bollocks

Bollocks is another word for 'shit', and it's used exactly the same way. The difference is the literal translation of the words. While 'shit' means poo, 'bollocks' is used to describe your testicles.

- ❖ Bugger

One of the most common words used by the British, bugger means to sodomize someone. The way you use it is to exclaim an unpleasant situation or annoyance

❖ Bloody Hell

Out of all British swear words, this is probably the one that's quickly being used by Americans. The word 'bloody' is also the foundational word that can be attached to other words to form a swear word, such as 'bloody moron' or to exclaim another word, like 'bloody brilliant!'

❖ Choad

Choad is just another word for penis and can be used similarly to the way the word 'dick' is used in America.

❖ Crikey

Some may argue that this isn't a swear word, but it's an important English word to recognized nevertheless. Crikey is often used to show astonishment and surprise, similar to the way the word 'Christ!' is used.

- ❖ Rubbish

Rubbish is what the British refers to as 'trash.' So when you tell someone their work is 'rubbish' it means that it's trash.

- ❖ Shag

To 'shag' means to have sex. Not incredibly offensive when you used it around your friends, but just a less direct way to describe fornication.

❖ Wanker

The word 'wank' means to masturbate, which means adding 'er' means you're calling someone a masturbater.

❖ Taking the piss

If someone from your team is being unproductive or just downright silly, you can say 'are you taking the piss?'

❖ Twat

Twat is translated to 'p*ssy' so you can imagine how this word can be colorfully used in many different situations.

Australian Swear Words (AU)

❖ Bloody Oath

Code for: 'F*ck Yeah!' Often used to show your immense support for something.

❖ Root

What 'shag' is to the British, the word 'root' is for Australians. Used very similarly.

❖ Get Stuffed

An easy substitute to tell someone to 'bugger off' or 'piss off.'

- ❖ Bugger me

This one may be a bit confusing since the word 'me' is used here. But it also means to 'get lost.' The more appropriate term would be 'bugger off'

- ❖ Fair suck of the sav

We had to end off our list of English curse words with this idiosyncratic one. The word "sav" is short for saveloy, or a red, seasoned sausage, and it's used when you want to say 'give me a fair chance or shot.'

English Dirty Words

Fuck – "Sex", or an Intensifier

That's right. Let's get it out in the open. There's that swear word which has all the oomph and intensity behind it. It can be used for sexual references, but it's most commonly used now as an intensifier to show your anger or irritation. In Ireland, we have a milder way of saying it with "feck". This one has also integrated into other languages, like Japanese, where speakers often say this word instead of one from their own language.

Prick – "Terrible/Rude Person"

A word used when someone is being obnoxious, stupid, or rude.

Bastard – "Illegitimate Child"

Originally meaning a child born out of wedlock, now it's used to call someone a jerk or to say a situation's unpleasant. You could also say "git" (pronounced with a hard G).

Bellend – "Penis Head"

Ah, so many dirty words are associated with certain body parts. This one refers to a penis, or is used to call someone an idiot. There's also knobend and dickhead.

Ass/Arse – "Butt"

Calling someone a jerk or a fool ("You asshole!") or saying you couldn't give a damn ("I don't give an arse" or "I can't be arsed").

Cunt – "Vagina"

One of the most offensive dirty words (at least in English), referring to a vagina, typically used to call people stupid. In the UK, this word alone can mean a movie is rated "18", so can only be seen by adults.

Balls – "Testicles"

Often thrown out there as a question of manliness or courage to do or not do something. "He doesn't have the balls to do it." or "He has some balls to say that." (Like "he has some nerve.") In the UK you might hear "bollocks" more often.

Shit – "Poop" or "Crap"

Now one of the most universal bad words there is in the English language. Shit is used in so many ways, like "piece of shit" to say something is worthless, or "shitty" as an adjective for something bad — like a "shitty day." "You don't know shit" means you don't know anything, but "you know your shit" means you know quite a lot! It's also used as an exclamation when something bad happens.

Irish Dirty Words

There are some really interesting ways to insult someone or curse in Irish – it gets pretty clever. But here's some dirty words you need to know:

Gobdaw – "Dumbass"

A gullible idiot. Like calling someone a "dumbass" or "twat".

Fecker – "Fucker"

Like I mentioned, "feck" is a milder form of "fuck", and the same is true for fecker. It's similar to "fucker", but a little "kinder".

Ráicleach – "Witch"

Or more accurate in this context: a loose woman, a lady of iffy morals, a slut.

Cúl Tóna – "Dickhead"

Used when someone's being a jerk.

Aiteann – "Cunt"

Another unsavoury word for lady parts, it most closely translates to "cunt" or "pussy" and it's one of the strongest words in Irish.

Téigh go dtí ifreann! – "Go to Hell!"

There are lots of creative variations of this one stemming from "devil" and "hell". But this is the classic for when you're really angry with someone.

Póg mo thóin. – "Kiss My Ass."

For when you really want to tell someone to suck it.

French Dirty Words

La belle langue is about to get a bit dirty!

Merde – "Shit"

Definitely the most common of all the French dirty words, it's used like "shit" in English. Your every day, all-situations curse word.

Putain – "Whore"

Although it means "whore", it's used more like "fuck". You can use it to express exasperation, exclamation, and as an adjective. You can even combine it with merde to create putain de merde — "fucking shit."

C'est des Conneries – "This is Bullshit"

Like in English, if you're feeling frustrated with a situation, you can call bullshit. Or, grumble about it to yourself in your target language.

Salope – "Bitch*

Also, "slut". It's a bit harsher than the English "bitch" which is sometimes used in a casual way.

Fils de Salope – "Son of a Bitch"

Obviously, use with care whenever you start referring to mothers. But you can use this as an exclamation like in English, too. Fils de pute ("son of a whore") is a common alternative.

T'as Pas de Couilles – "You Don't Have the Balls"

Want to call someone out on their bluff? Tell them they don't have to balls to go through with it.

Je M'en Fous – "I Don't Give a Shit"

When you're looking for an eloquent way to express your lack of shits to give, here's your phrase!

Osti de Calisse de Tabarnak (Quebec only) – "Goddamn Motherfucking Shit!"

This is the mother of all curses in Quebec. Each word on its own (osti, calisse and tabarnak) is itself a swear word that can be used individually, but they combine to form a phrase that will have your mother washing your mouth out with soap in no time flat.

Spanish Dirty Words

Such a passionate language is bound to have colourful dirty words. Here are some creative ways to express frustration:

Mierda – "Shit"

This literally refers to faeces but can be used in any situation to express frustration.

Váyase a la Mierda – "Fuck off"

Also using "mierda" but in a stronger way. Could also be translated as, "Go fuck yourself."

Que te Folle un Pez – "I Hope You Get Fucked By a Fish"

I have no idea where this one started, but talk about a creative way to tell someone off!

Puto – "Fucking"

Used as an adjective, like Mira este puto – "Look at this fucking guy."

Verga – "Cock" or "Prick"

Basically, an arrogant idiot.

Cojones – "Balls"

It wouldn't be right to leave this one off the list. Men love to talk about los cojones and whether another person has them, or rather the courage and muster. Sometimes you'll hear Tienes cojones – "You have balls" – like in English.

Coño – "Cunt"

This one has various meanings, depending on where you hear it. It can also be "twat" or even "damn" in Spain. It's not always considered as offensive as the English equivalent, depending which country you're in and who you're talking to, but use it carefully just in case.

Italian Dirty Words

You may know a few inappropriate hand gestures in Italian – so here are some passionate expressions to go with them.

Cazzo – "Dick"

Also "fuck" or "shit", it's the common swear word for everything in Italian.

Che Palle! – "What balls!"

When someone has a lot of nerve, that's what this line is for.

Tette – "Tits"

I can just picture you giggling at this one.

Stronzo – "Asshole"

Or, stronza for a woman.

Fanculo – "Fuck"

You can use it as an exclamation, or to express your anger with someone.

Vaffanculo – "Fuck You"

This is definitely one you'll see with some not-so-nice hand gestures, and it ranks amongst the strongest terms in Italian.

Pompinara – "Cocksucker"

A strong noun to call someone in your wrath. Keep in mind, these may be fighting words to Italians.

German Dirty Words

German has some amazingly descriptive words for all occasions… And swear words are no exception.

Arschgesicht – "Ass Face"

Yes, "ass face", or a little harsher – "fuck face." It's a pretty intense (and humorous) insult.

Scheißkopf – "Shithead"

Basically, a "dumbass" or "idiot" you can't stand.

Küss meinen Arsch – "Kiss My Ass"

A handy phrase for when someone's getting on your last nerve.

Verpiss Dich! – "Fuck Off!"

When you want to get the hell away from someone.

Zur Hölle mit… – "To Hell With…"

Like, Zur Hölle mit ihnen – "To hell with 'em!"

Wichser – "Wanker"

Like "prick" or "asshole," and used the same way.

Arschgeige – "Dickhead"

Similar to Arschgesicht, but this one translates to "ass fiddle" which is just an incredible insult.

Portuguese Dirty Words

While there are some differences between Brazilian Portuguese and European Portuguese, these are some standard bad words from the language.

Cabra / Cabrão – "Bastard" or "Fucker"

Cabra is feminine, and Cabrão is masculine, and both are offensive.

Monte de Merda – "Piece of Shit"

Merda means "shit", so you can use it as you would that word.

Caralho – "Dick"

While it means penis, cock, or dick, it's used more like "fuck." You can also say *foda-se which is used like an exclamation when something bad happens.

Vai Para o Caralho – "Go Fuck Yourself"

For when you're really pissed off.

Rego Do Cu – "Ass Crack"

A noun for someone who's being very irritating or arrogant.

Puta Que Pariu – "Holy Shit"

Used as an interjection or exclamation to express surprise (and often slips out in the moment).

Chupa-mos – "Suck it"

Perhaps a bit nicer way to say Vai para o caralho.

Russian Dirty Words

Russian curse words are quite an art form. They start with a few basic words that morph into thousands of variations and ways to offend someone.

Хуй (Khui) – "Dick"

While it translates to "dick", it transforms into a catch-all dirty word, like for the next phrase….

Хуй тебé! (Khui tebé!) – "Fuck You!"

Хуй is often the root of all major insults in Russian.

Сучка (Suchka) – "Little Bitch"

A noun for when someone's pissed you off.

Обосрáться (Obosrat'sya) – "Shit" or "Crapping One's Pants"

This can refer to the object "crap" or the action "crapping oneself." Quite the lovely image!

Не будь жо́пой! (Ne bud' zhopoy!) – "Don't Be an Asshole!"

When you need to tell someone to lay off.

бля́дь (blyad') – "Whore"

Another catch-all word, this one is used as an exclamation like "damn" or "shit." But also used to call a woman a "slut" or a man a "dickhead".

Да еба́л я э́то! (Da yebal ya eto!) – "I Fucked Up!"

Or "I don't fucking care anymore!" for when you're exasperated, or messed up.

Chinese Dirty Words

Chinese has some very interesting ways to insult someone, so I'm going to start right out with my favourite:

王八蛋 (Wáng Bā Dàn) – "Tortoise Egg"

Yes, this is a highly insulting phrase in Chinese, and basically equates to "bastard" in English. The interesting thing about this phrase is it's become such a common bad word that it spurred tons of other "egg" related insults.

混蛋 (Hún Dàn) – "Mixed Egg"

This is like throwing out a "yo mama" insult because it means that the family line is "mixed" or messed up from promiscuity. Since the family name and ancestry is huge, this is a major insult. But its English equivalent is closest to "prick."

狗屁 (Gǒu Pì) – "Dog Fart"

You read that right: "dog fart". It's used like "bullshit". As in 放你妈的狗屁 (fàng nǐ mā de gǒu pì) – "Your mom's dog fart" or "That's bullshit."

混帐 (Hùn zhàng) – "Git"

Also means "bastard" and is a major insult.

他妈的 (Tā mā de) – "Fuck"

Like in English, it's used as an exclamation or intensifier.

去你的 (Qù nǐ de) – "Shut the Fuck Up"

Or "screw you" and "fuck off". It's actually a bit milder than it sounds in English.

我肏 (Wǒ Cào) – "Holy Shit"

Used when you're equally surprised and impressed.

Japanese Dirty Words

Japanese bad words don't always have the same "oomph" they do in other languages, because giving offense in Japanese can be so nuanced. But here are some common offensive words:

くそ (Kuso) – "Shit" or "Fuck"

The most versatile dirty word in Japanese, kuso means "shit", "damn" or "fuck" and is used the same as in English.

やりまん (Yariman) – "Slut"

Used when calling someone promiscuous, and it's highly insulting. There's also the male version — やりちん (yarichin).

くそったれ (Kusottare) – "Shithead"

The equivalent of calling someone "Motherfucker" in English. It's one of the stronger words in Japanese.

ぶす (Busu) – "Ugly Hag"

While this is a pretty mild word comparatively, it's a common insult meaning "ugly woman". You'll hear rude kids sometimes call women this in anime (and real life).

死ねえ (Shi'ne) – "Die!"

A popular one you might've heard if you watch shonen anime, it's the harshest way to tell someone "Die!" But when you're not in a ninja battle to the death, it more accurately translates to "Go to hell" in everyday life.

くたばれ、ボケ (Kutabare, boke) – "Fuck Off, Idiot"

Although it's a bit stronger than "idiot" implies in English. "Fuck off, you piece of shit" is a closer translation for this one.

Korean Dirty Words

There are lots of fun slang and dirty expressions in Korean, even some silly ones from kids' shows like calling someone 빵구똥구 (bbang-gu-ddong-gu – "poopy fart").

아, 씨발 (Ah, Sshi-bal) – "Ah, Fuck"

It can be used the same way as in English.

씨방새 (Sshi-bang-sae) – "Fuck You"

Here's the intense way to tell someone to leave you alone in Korean.

개새(Gae-sae) – "SOB"

"Son of a bitch" or "SOB". It's a shortened way to literally say "a dog's offspring."

년(Nyeon) – "Bitch"

There are lots of other expressions that stem from this one, but this is your standard insult.

좆(Jot) – "Penis"

Literally meaning a penis or dick. But it's used in many fun sayings, like…

좆같은놈/년(Jeot-gat-eun-nom/nyeon) – "You bastard/bitch"

Also like saying "you're shitty," but would more accurately translate to "bastard" or "bitch" in English.

아, 좆같네(Ah, jot-gat-ne) – "It's fucked up"

It means "It's like a dick" but the English translation would be closer to "It's fucked up."

CONCLUSION

Now Go Learn Some Bleeping Useful Words

Got that out of your system? You can go swear like a sailor in languages from around the world now! But if you get yourself in trouble using them, you're on your own! Don't forget to go learn some polite words to make up for the vulgarity, like essential phrases in other languages.

Printed in Great Britain
by Amazon